COFFEE with God

Volume 4

On the Road

Becky Alexander, June Foster, Michael Loudiana, PhD,
Bonita Y. McCoy, Suzanne D. Nichols,
Lisa Worthey Smith

Kerysso Press

REL012020   RELIGION / Christian Living / Devotional
REL012150   RELIGION/ Christian Living / Devotional Journal

paperback ISBN 979-8-989552-0-1

Kerysso Press

PREFACE

We each have a road to travel today. We might be leaving home for college, on a daily commute, in transit to a vacation destination, or on an unexpected, and perhaps unwelcome, life detour. Every choice along our path today can bring us closer to God or detour us away from Him.

COFFEE with God On the Road fuels us with the Word of God, a short devotion, and a prayer, to set our GPS toward Him. Whether we're faced with tempting distractions on a familiar road or trying to find the way on an unfamiliar path, together, we can press on toward our finish line.

Look for the music notes to find songs that will keep you focused during the journey. We're praying every mile and each step leads you closer to Him.

Blessings,

Lisa Worthey Smith

This book is dedicated

to everyone on a journey.

Whether you are launching out on a fresh adventure,

or nearing the finish line,

we're praying God will be with you

each step of the way.

When those steps become uncertain or difficult,

we pray God will lead you

with His gentle hand

to places of peace and joy.

We pray He gives you opportunities along the way

to share with others about His unending love.

CONTENTS

TITLE

COFFEE with God

Volume 4

On the Road

Day 1

 An Earthly Goal and a Heavenly Goal

My goal is that they may be encouraged in heart and united in love,
so that they may have the full riches of complete understanding,
in order that they may know the mystery of God,
namely, Christ,
in whom are hidden all the treasures
of wisdom and knowledge.
Colossians 2:2-3 (NIV)

I'm a State-Chaser—a person with the goal of crossing all fifty state lines.

I began my quest in 2009. Reminiscing with my parents, I listed the states from my childhood trips. Driving to Disney World from Ohio included Kentucky, Tennessee, Georgia, and Florida. Taking my grandfather to the Mayo Clinic covered Indiana, Illinois, Wisconsin, and Minnesota. We traveled through Mississippi and Arkansas to visit Uncle Otis at Fort Polk in Louisiana. My prosthetic arms were made in Grand Rapids, Michigan. When I added other adventures as a teen and adult, the list grew to twenty-five states.

Not a bad starting point. Twenty-five down, twenty-five to go.

During the next seven years, I passed a state line sign every chance I got. If my job as a tour director took me anywhere close to a place I needed on the list, I rented a car in my free time, drove over the line, explored a bit, and drove back. And by the morning of May 16, 2016, I cruised on icy waters into beautiful Alaska ... State #50 ... the completion of my State-Chaser goal.

My earthly goal provided travel fun and happy memories, but it carried no eternal value. That's where my second goal comes in, the one I call my heavenly goal. Colossians 2:2 articulates it best: *My goal is that they may be encouraged in heart.* I want to invest this life in uplifting others and giving them hope through Jesus!

Encouragement can come in many forms. I've discovered the cheapest and easiest is a smile. People get so used to passing others without interaction that a smile catches them off guard, in a good way. They seem appreciative of the moment of friendliness.

Spoken words of encouragement can take root and linger for a lifetime. Recently, a friend repeated a positive statement back to me that I'd said to her long ago. I have no memory of saying it, yet I'm glad I did.

Written messages can offer encouragement, again and again. Tucked in the console of my Beetle, a lavender paper reads: "I luv u grammy." Though the edges are curled with age and the ink has faded from the sun, the inspiration remains fresh for each new view.

Meeting a need can give hope and encouragement in the name of Jesus. A teacher friend puts boxes of cereal and packs of fruit in kids' backpacks when she suspects they came to school without breakfast. A small gift can have a big impact on someone's day.

What are your "just for fun" earthly goals? Consider crossing a few state lines. What are your heavenly goals, the ones with eternal value? I invite you to become an official encourager today.

Dear Jesus,

Thank You for sending encouragement my way often. Help me notice those around me who could use a smile or an uplifting word. And make me super-sensitive to the needs of others.

In Your name I pray, amen.

Becky Alexander

♪♫ "The Great Adventure" by Steven Curtis Chapman

MY NOTES

Day 2

Shortcut

It is not good to have zeal without knowledge,
nor to be hasty and miss the way.
Proverbs 19:2 (NIV)

We arrived at Newport News Campground around four o'clock in the afternoon on Day Two of a ten-day camping trip. My husband Roger and I were eager to spend the next five days enjoying our oldest son and his family living near Newport News, Virginia.

A map provided by the campground's office marked our assigned site. Following directional signs through the thickly wooded acreage, we crept along the leaf-strewn paths as acorns, pinecones, and sticks crunched and popped under the truck and camper tires.

We found Site #16 in a picturesque setting overlooking Lee Hall Reservoir. However, several unsuccessful attempts to situate the camper safely and efficiently on the site left us with no option but to choose another one. To do so required a return trip to the office.

Realizing the approaching sunset would bring additional challenges to the set-up process, we wasted no time trekking back up the winding path.

The woods opened to a paved area behind the office. Unsure of where to park our thirty-foot-long rig, Roger decided to drive around to the front entrance where we'd initially stopped for check-in. As he navigated the turn preparing to take the right-hand lane, he slowed, realizing a median divided the way from camp road to highway with no cross-over to the front of the office from the exit lane.

He was faced with two options: continue to the exit and merge into the five o'clock highway traffic and drive until he found a suitable place to turn around; or, go the wrong way a few yards and make a tight turn into the parking area. Roger chose the shortcut.

As he fully committed to his wrong-way travel, a vehicle turned off the highway onto the camp road. With little time to safely clear the way, he rushed his planned approach. Consequently, he jumped the curb, rutting the grassy area, and rode up on the sidewalk. The truck's front bumper tapped two trash barrels, spinning them out of place before we jostled to a stop. Somehow, he avoided scraping the camper along a large pine tree.

Embarrassed and aggravated with himself, Roger jumped from the truck to survey the mess. He straightened the trash barrels and entered the office to confess his blunder.

Thankfully, the manager responded kindly and granted us permission to set up on a more suitable site.

I can see my life's paths in my husband's choices. I, too, have panicked in the face of an oncoming crisis. I've attempted a shortcut to my goals because the way seemed easier than navigating the heavy traffic of anxiety and self-doubt. I've jumped the curb and rutted the ground of cherished relationships when I've rushed to assumptions or spoken without forethought. At times, my walk of faith has left me embarrassed and aggravated with myself. However, when I confess my wrong to God, He responds kindly and brings me back to the proper path.

Merciful Father,

I confess with the psalmist David, "The Lord is good ... He shows the proper path to those who go astray. He leads the humble in what is right, teaching them His way. Lead me by Your truth and teach me."

I come to You in Jesus' name, amen.

Suzanne D. Nichols

"Every Move I Make, I Make in You" by Integrity Music

MY NOTES

Recalculating

But the Holy Spirit produces this kind of fruit in our lives:
love, joy, peace, patience, kindness, goodness, faithfulness,
gentleness, and self-control.
Galatians 5:22 (NLT)

It was a Friday that felt more like a Monday. One of those Mondays that songwriters sing about on the radio. Manic, rainy, where everything that could go wrong does.

My middle son entered the kitchen and announced that he couldn't find his left shoe. I swallowed the frustration stirring in me and bit back the words of accusation that perched on the tip of my tongue. He stood hugging his right shoe against his chest, but the left one had somehow disappeared between Karate last night and the rising of the sun this morning. "Mom, I put it in the basket by the back door just like you told me." He pointed with the tennis shoe in his hand toward the basket.

I suppressed the urge to roll my eyes. "Fine," I huffed. "I'll come help you look for it." I stopped before going upstairs and pressed the button on the coffee maker. This was definitely a two-cup morning.

Ten minutes later, I returned to the kitchen to discover that my Mr. Coffee had exploded all over the counter. The grounds swam in the dark pools that dripped over the edge to the floor, staining my new kitchen mat a rich shade of brown.

After a swift clean-up of the mess, three shouts up the stairs, and a mad dash to the van, I had the crew belted in their seats ready to head to Friday classes at our homeschool community. We had just enough time to get there without being late.

But to my complete surprise, the city had started repaving the potholes on the road leading to the school. When I had to take a detour, my GPS squawked, "recalculating, recalculating." Every few feet the female voice reminded me that she had to recalculate the route since we were sent in a whole new direction.

Sometimes in my daily walk, I have to recalculate my feelings when life puts roadblocks in my way. Like my GPS, I must find an alternative route to deal with life's little hiccups and not let my feelings of irritation and anger control the situation.

In Galatians, we read the fruit of the Spirit includes love, joy, patience, and self-control. I certainly didn't feel loving or patient that Friday morning when life seemed like an uphill battle. But my GPS reminded me, I could recalculate my feelings and bring them in line with God's Word, changing the whole outcome of my day.

Thankfully, the day and my attitude got better after a little talk with Father God. Taking the GPS's good advice, I recalculated my emotions and decided to go a different direction letting the fruit of the Spirit work in me. It wasn't easy, but God showed his faithfulness as I worked to align my emotions with His Spirit.

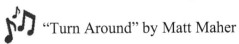

Dear Father,

Thank you for the Fruit of the Holy Spirit that is in each one of us. Please help me to let Your Spirit work in my life each day and on the days that seem impossible, the ones filled with heartache and challenges, let Your Spirit fill me with Your love.

In Jesus's name, amen.

Bonita Y. McCoy

🎵 "Turn Around" by Matt Maher

MY NOTES

Day 4

 **Scenic View Pullover Ahead**

This is the day that the Lord has made;
let us rejoice and be glad in it.
Psalm 118:24 (ESV)

I enjoy planning travel adventures. In fact, I may like to plan more than I like to travel. So, when my wife, who is much more spontaneous than I, wants to pull over and enjoy an unplanned scenic view, I sort of dread it. It's hard for me to be in the moment and enjoy the view when I keep thinking about my schedule and to-do list.

I think that's true for a lot of people. When we're not working, we're busy thinking about what needs to get done—some of us anyway.

Yet God gave us so much more than meaningful work. He gave us an incredibly delightful creation, and He yearns for us to stop and simply be present in it with Him. He wants us to experience the joy of seeing a beautiful waterfall, trees full of colorful birds, or a stunning field of flowers.

My older brother Tim was a master of living in the moment and experiencing joy. He would wake up at 5:00 a.m. and start singing at the top of his lungs. That was his way of telling the world that he was ready to start the day. It was also my father's signal to come and help him get into his wheelchair.

Tim loved music and had amassed a large collection of 45s—seven-inch vinyl records spun at forty-five revolutions per minute, with one song on each side. He joined a choir at the institution where he lived, and they performed concerts and even cut a record album of their own.

Tim was physically and mentally challenged due to a birth defect, but he didn't let it define him. I always looked forward to the weekends when Mom and Dad would bring him home. I enjoyed playing cards and checkers with him. I loved his joyful personality. It was like a little bit of heaven.

Tim had some trials in his life, but at times I envied him. He saw only the good in everyone. He didn't complain, gossip, or boast and maintained a childlike wonder and delight. Jesus said, "Whoever then humbles himself as this child, he is the greatest in the kingdom of heaven."

Tim left this world far too early. Every year, starting when he was born, Tim's doctor would tell our parents he wouldn't live another year. He lived to the ripe old age of 32, and I know he is singing with Jesus now.

There is great beauty in this world and universe. Heaven must be even more beautiful. I imagine it is filled with beautiful souls, and those child-like people who have the greatest rewards.

So, when you encounter something or someone God has put in your path, whether it is beautiful scenery or someone like Tim, remember to stop, be present with God, and experience the joy God has in store for you.

Dear Lord God,

Thank You for the beauty of Your creation, and for all the wonderful people You have placed in my life. Help me to remember to put aside my busyness and experience the child-like joy You intended for me.

In Jesus' name, amen.

Michael Loudiana, PhD

♪♫ "Joy" by Highlands Worship

MY NOTES

Day 5

Dead End

If we confess our sins, he is faithful and just
and will forgive us our sins and purify us from all unrighteousness.
1 John 1:9 (NIV)

I snuck a glance at my watch. Late. Would I make it to my first chiropractor appointment after I injured my back? I braked at the red light and then pressed the gas pedal when the traffic signal turned green. I sighed in relief. The next turn to the left and I'd arrive at my destination. I flipped on my blinkers and maneuvered the turn but not before I spotted the sign that stated *dead end.*

Uh, oh. Not this street but the next one to the left. But I'd already turned. Nothing to do but find a place to circle around.

Later, when I returned home, the analogy dawned. The route I'd gone had taken me somewhere I didn't want to go. I wouldn't have seen the chiropractor and could've suffered with a sore back for months.

Here's the good news. I turned around and made my way to the doctor's office. But what if finding another way had been impossible?

Thankfully, for months during the pandemic, I avoided becoming ill. Then one day I felt yucky and decided to take one of my home tests. My mouth dropped open when I saw the little red line next to the blue. The next day, I went to the neighborhood quick-care clinic. They confirmed. I had Covid.

Lying on my outdoor patio couch, I closed my eyes and began to pray asking the Lord if He planned to take me home that day as I certainly felt bad enough. In that moment, I realized that when the time comes, there will be no fear of dying. That day will be wonderful. I will pass on into a beautiful existence and dwell with the Lord forever.

The Bible says that no one is fit to reside in Heaven because of Adam and Eve's rebellion in the Garden of Eden. But God is loving and compassionate so He made a way for us. He sent His Son Jesus Christ to the earth to live a sinless life and die on a cross. By His death, He paid the debt that I owed God, yet there was no cost to me. I only reached out and received His free gift. I'm forgiven of my sins and can live with Him forever and ever.

I don't know exactly what the next life will look like, but I'm convinced that Heaven will be glorious because I will be in God's presence.

For many years of my life, I took dead-end roads. If I had not asked the Savior into my life to redeem me before I died, I cringe to think of the consequences. Unlike the day I went to the chiropractor, I wouldn't have been able to change course.

Are you walking down a dead-end road? It's so simple to turn around, but don't wait until it's too late.

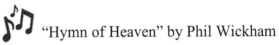

Lord,

I confess I'm not worthy to stand in Your presence, so I receive the sacrifice the Lord Jesus Christ made for me so I can spend all eternity with You.

In Jesus name, amen.

June Foster

"Hymn of Heaven" by Phil Wickham

MY NOTES

Day 6

Route 66

Only be strong and very courageous;
be careful to do according to all the law
which Moses My servant commanded you;
do not turn from it to the right or to the left,
so that you may have success wherever you go.
Joshua 1:7 (NASB95)

Route 66, established in 1926, connected hundreds of small towns and eight states from Chicago to Los Angeles, California. During the devastating Dust Bowl, desperate farming families packed their belongings and headed down the road hoping for a new start with new land. Steinbeck dubbed it the Mother Road in his novel *Grapes of Wrath* about that era.

As more families purchased automobiles, they also bought maps to guide them in navigating roads, cities, and points of interest. The paper maps usually displayed the major roads of an entire state when fully open and detailed maps of cities on the other side. If travelers read and followed their maps and road signs, they could reach their desired destination.

In the Scripture passage above, God reminded the Israelites of the importance of staying on the path He laid out for them. His laws were their roadmap guiding them on the road to blessings, and away from destruction.

They had seen miracles from God during and after their rescue from Egyptian slavery but lost faith several times. Without following His roadmap, they wandered in a desert for forty years before they could enter the promised land He described as flowing with milk and honey.

When it was time for them to cross the Jordan River to go into their new homeland, God warned them to remember the laws He had given them, and not stray to the right or the left. He told them to speak about and concentrate on His Word so they would remember to do the things that pleased God. He promised if they did, their way would be successful.

At first, they were diligent to seek God and obey His commands. They conquered their enemies and settled in the land He promised them. Other times, rather than follow His commands fully, they strayed after enticements and disobeyed His law. A few steps off course here and there, their faith faltered and they allowed temptations to distract them from God and His Word.

We have God's Word, our roadmap, preserved in sixty-six books—the Bible. The more we stay on His Route 66 (the 66 books of the Bible), speak of His Word, and meditate on it, the more it becomes a part of our lives. When His Word connects our heart, soul, and mind, our thoughts can focus on Him and we can follow in faith. When we diligently study His guide, we are more likely to steer clear of temptations and remain on the path He wants for us—a righteous route leading to blessings.

Dear Father,

Thank You for giving us Your Word to navigate the path before us. We want to be faithful and follow You in every step.

Help us to keep Your Word near to our minds, in our thoughts, and on our lips, so we can clearly see and follow Your righteous way among the bumps, distractions, and curves in the roads.

In Jesus' name, amen.

Lisa Worthey Smith

 "Thy Word" by Amy Grant

MY NOTES

Day 7

Mechanic on Duty

Trust in the Lord with all your heart
and lean not on your own understanding;
in all your ways acknowledge Him,
and He will make your paths straight.
Proverbs 3:5-6 (NIV)

"I'm telling you, Honey, there's something wrong with this truck," my husband Roger moaned as we made our way along Kentucky's Interstate 24. He'd been saying this in a variety of ways but with the same anxious tone before we'd reached our first destination in Virginia one week earlier. Three days remained in our ten-day camping trip with our new twenty-foot travel trailer.

Steady showers accompanied us as we left West Virginia that morning. Rain, grooved pavement, and the truck tires harmonized in a high-pitched whine all the way from the I-24 of West Virginia to "The Double A" of Kentucky. I called attention to this acoustic phenomenon as an explanation for the noise.

Roger pulled off the highway and rolled down his window. "Nope," he declared. "We left that grooved pavement behind when we crossed from West Virginia into Kentucky. This road is smooth as glass—no grooves to cause that roaring whine I've been hearing."

As we traveled on, the roar grew louder.

Roger's careful study of the highway map that morning informed him that many miles still lay between us and the day's destination. He confided that, if we were to break down, he feared we could be at the mercy of untrustworthy service providers.

"Loving Father," he prayed aloud. "Please guide us to a reputable mechanic. Soon."

No more than five minutes later he caught sight of the upper half of a large metal building high on a hill. Vehicles and U-Haul rentals lined the yard. The three open bays of L & L Auto Service beckoned us upward.

Roger drove the steep, rutted drive to a flat spot in the yard. I remained in the truck, praying while I admired the undulating, green hills of Tollsboro, Kentucky.

When he returned, his words tumbled out with joy and relief as he described his instant bond with the Christian men he'd met inside.

He unhooked the camper and drove the truck into one of the bays. A mechanic's inspection confirmed worn-out gears in the rear axle. They located a replacement an hour away in Cincinnati, Ohio and scheduled the installation for the following morning. As sunset approached, we settled in to "boondock" (camp without electricity, water, or sewer) right where we sat.

I've come to expect a memorable event from each camping trip we take, but this one shines with wonder and gratitude. God led us to the perfect place for our need at the appointed time of our need.

Proverbs 3:5-6 came to mind that day with a clear understanding of its commands and promises: If we trust God with all our being and resist the tendency to view life through the narrow lens of human limitations or self-sufficiency, but choose to open our souls to recognize God's perspective, we will more readily see how He protects and provides in times of need, how He guides and directs in times of uncertainty, how He tests and teaches in times of crisis.

Loving Father,

I rest in Your faithfulness and rejoice in the sweet assurance that You do care, do hear, and do answer prayer.

For Jesus' sake and in His name I pray, amen.

Suzanne D. Nichols

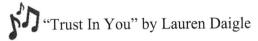 "Trust In You" by Lauren Daigle

MY NOTES

Day 8

Bump

Do not boast about tomorrow,
for you do not know what a day may bring forth.
Proverbs 27:1 (NIV)

One summer, I signed up my two older boys for Vacation Bible School at the church we attended. We normally traveled during the summer break, but for the first time, we'd be home, and they could participate. I was thrilled. I had always wanted them to be involved in this activity since I had such fond memories of my own experience.

On day three of VBS, I received a call from the children's minister. Could I come? My son was hurt.

Strapping the youngest into his car seat, I sped twenty minutes down the road to see what was wrong. When I arrived, both sons and the director stood on the sidewalk waiting for me. My middle son, who was eight, cradled his right arm across his belly.

The director explained what had happened. The accident involved a bouncy slide, a gym floor, and a teenager who had helped to bump him down the slide so he wouldn't get stuck.

One big bump too many and off my son flew to the gym floor hitting the metal border with his elbow.

Apologizing, the director helped me get him into the front seat. We set off for the emergency room forty minutes away. Once in an exam room, the doctor ordered an x-ray and confirmed that his arm was indeed broken above his elbow. Due to the location of the fracture, he'd need surgery to put in a pin to hold the bones in place.

It was a long six weeks of healing for my middle son. Ice packs, slings, and taking it slow were not in his plan or mine for the summer. His broken arm turned out to be a bigger bump than we'd expected.

But that experience taught me even when we are doing something worthwhile and God-directed, there are going to be bumps along the way.

In the Scripture, Solomon admonished us not to boast about tomorrow because we have no idea what a day may hold. And that summer proved God's Word true again. We don't know what a day, a month, or a year may hold or what bumps may be present.

Some difficulties may be like the speed bumps we find in parking lots where we know about them and can brace for them, and others may be like the bumps on the bouncy slide, unexpected and painful. But there is one thing for sure, there will be bumps along the journey.

So, if you are busy doing what God has given you to do and a bump comes your way, don't despair. It's only a bump to you. God already knew what the day would hold, and He is more than able to equip you for the tasks He has given you to do. As Philippians 4:13 states, "For God is working in you, giving you the desire and the power to do what pleases Him."

Bumps and all.

Father,

Thank You for this wonderful life, a gift I open one day at a time. Please fill my days with Your will and watch over me and my family as the bumps come our way. May You use each experience to draw me nearer to You.

In Jesus' name, amen.

Bonita Y. McCoy

♫ "Hold On" by Katy Nichole

MY NOTES

Day 9

Rough Road

Do to others as you would have them do to you.

Luke 6:31 (NIV)

I hung up the phone with our realtor. Everything was going according to plan. The house had sold, the papers were signed, and my husband and I were to pick up our new RV the next day. We were ready to explore the US once again.

Were we modern-day nomads? I supposed so. After moving every few years while my husband served in the army, we were used to being on the go. We had to travel again before we got too old.

My husband had dealt with bladder cancer the previous year but had had a couple of negative cystoscopies. We were in the clear. I accompanied him to his urologist appointment that Valentine's Day believing it would be the last visit to the doctor for a while.

When the doctor informed us the cancer was back, we were stunned.

"Stay where you are and begin treatments," the doctor advised.

We needed to remain in our hometown of Cullman, Alabama. What would we do now? Our house was sold. We'd committed to buying a new RV.

Our agent warned us of possible repercussions. The buyers could sue for breach of contract and demand we complete the sale anyway. They could ask for repayment of the money they'd already put into the sale. We'd have to find another house here in Cullman or move to another town and locate a new urologist. But she promised to call the buyers' agent and see what she could work out.

We prayed and left the entire matter in the Lord's hands. We clung to the scripture in Romans that says, "And we know that in all things God works for the good of those who love him, who have been called according to his purpose" (Romans 8:28 NIV). A couple of hours later, our agent called with news. I gulped and held on to the chair as I listened, barely comprehending her words.

The buyers wanted nothing from us except one thing. They wanted to come to our house and pray for us. God's grace and mercy had prevailed. These precious people were God's own and lived by His word.

Later the same day, a sedan rolled up in our driveway. The man and his wife emerged from the car. Though I'd never met either before,

I ran to the lady and hugged her. Then when I stepped toward the husband, I discovered he was visually challenged. The recollection of the four of us holding hands in our driveway is permanently seared into my memory.

If ever I saw the hand of God at work, it was that day. This dear couple showed the genuine love of God to us. Even today, we keep in touch by text. Anytime I have a prayer need, they are willing and ready to lift the request up to the Lord.

They are still looking for a house but want one in our neighborhood. Since they don't want to build, I'm praying for one of the homes near us to go on sale soon. Our neighborhood would be blessed to have such godly neighbors as these two people.

Lord,

Thank You for guiding us when the road gets rough and by placing people before us who show Your love. In Jesus' name, amen.

June Foster

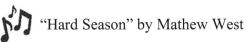 "Hard Season" by Mathew West

35

MY NOTES

Road Hazard

In Your unfailing love You will lead the people You have redeemed.
Exodus 15:13a (NIV)

Anticipation of a full week of camping had me double-checking our supplies and packing extras that Monday morning. My husband Roger had already performed his usual thorough inspections of his pickup truck and our twenty-foot travel trailer. We were ready to roll.

Our sights were set on one of our favorite get-away spots, a small, quaint campground only two-and-one-half hours from home. And, with plans for a family reunion later in the week, the park also offered a convenient gathering place in a pleasant, natural setting.

About fifty miles from our destination, we spotted a large chunk of tire tread in the center of our lane a few yards ahead. With interstate traffic passing us in the left lane, Roger was forced to continue in the right lane and straddle the road hazard. As the pickup passed over the mass, we heard—and felt—a "clunk, clunk."

Roger glanced in the rearview and side mirrors but noted no damage to the travel trailer in tow behind us.

We'd logged another ten miles when an eighteen-wheeler pulled alongside us in the left lane. A passenger in the truck's cab waved and pointed toward our camper as the driver repeatedly honked his horn.

Roger responded with a thumbs-up and guided our rig to the shoulder of the road. A quick inspection revealed the reason for the trucker's warning—smoke billowed from all four wheels. The errant tire tread had snagged the trailer's break-away safety switch causing the brakes to lock up. (A break-away switch applies a controlled braking action for a trailer should it become unhitched from the tow vehicle.)

After the brakes cooled a bit, Roger reconnected the switch and we cautiously traveled the few remaining miles to the campground.

"If only I could have gone around that big ole thing," he moaned as we rode on. "I was boxed in and had no choice."

~~~

The children of Israel faced a "no choice" situation as they stood at the shore of the Red Sea with Pharaoh's entire army closing in behind them. Pharaoh pushed his troops, horses, and all the chariots of Egypt toward the sea, believing he had his former slaves boxed in. Pressing closer, Pharaoh seemed determined to drown them or chase them back to Egypt through the desert.

The Israelites cried out in fear, certain of their fate. But God had a plan to display His glory and show Himself mighty to save. His children had only to respond in faith and step into the water.

Perhaps they were compelled onward by both fear and faith. I confess to feeling a similar conflict as we faced that chunk of tire tread. But God guided us over the obstacle and beyond it. We didn't wreck and the camper didn't catch on fire. Roger was able to replace the ruined brakes at the campsite without altering our family gathering. We added another memory to our collection of adventures and, like the Israelites, recorded undeniable evidence of God's ability to show Himself mighty to save.

O Great Deliverer,

When fear and hazards box me in, stir my soul with the testimony of the psalmist, David. With him I will declare, "The Lord is my strength and my shield; my heart trusts in Him, and I am helped."

In the saving name of Jesus I pray, amen.

Suzanne D. Nichols

 "Evidence" by Josh Baldwin

MY NOTES

Day 11

Merging Traffic

Be kind and compassionate to one another,
forgiving each other,
just as in Christ God forgave you.
Ephesians 4:32 (NIV)

When driving down the Interstate, I give cars in front of me lots of room to merge smoothly into my lane from the entrance ramp before their lane ends. Often a car will wait until the last possible moment before they dart in front of me. I don't know whether I should be annoyed or amused by their lack of planning.

As we travel along the highway of life, we encounter many people who merge into and out of our lives. Some of these people we encounter for only a moment, and some are life-long companions. We may tend to give more grace to people we know and love.

It seems so easy to judge strangers, even though Jesus instructed us not to judge others. We may not even realize we are doing it. It may show up as impatience, like when the car in front of us dares to impede our travel.

When driving, it is easy to think of the other cars as impersonal things and not think of the people inside of them. I once drove behind a car that was not maintaining a consistent speed. It kept speeding up and slowing down. As I passed, I noticed that the driver was a young lady with two small children in the car. She was on the phone crying. I didn't know her situation, but she needed my compassion and prayers, not my impatience. So, I whispered a prayer as I rolled by.

Another thing I need to remember is that God is gracious and has forgiven me of much wrongdoing. Jesus died for my unrighteousness and even forgave those who had betrayed Him, like Peter.

After Jesus was arrested and the soldiers led Him away to His trial, Peter followed at a distance. When others recognized Peter as a disciple of Jesus, he denied it—not once, but three times. *Just as he was speaking, the rooster crowed. The Lord turned and looked straight at Peter. Then Peter remembered the word the Lord had spoken to him: "Before the rooster crows today, you will disown me three times." And he went outside and wept bitterly* (Luke 22:60 – 62, NIV). Peter repented and even though he betrayed the son of God, Jesus forgave him. Peter was able to merge back onto the narrow path that leads to heaven.

My sins are no less than Peter's betrayal and there is nothing I can do to cover them. Yet, Christ died for me and paid the price for my sins, and he died for all these other people that I may think of as hindrances, or not think of at all.

As we drive down the highway of life, we can take a few moments to slow down and notice others around us. Be compassionate, kind, and forgiving to those who are merging in front of you.

Dear Lord God,

Thank You for Your amazing grace. You didn't have to save us for eternity, but You did because of Your love for us. Help us to be compassionate, kind, and forgiving to others, just as You are forgiving to us.

In Jesus' name, amen.

Michael Loudiana, PhD

♫ "This is Amazing Grace" by Beth Gagliano

MY NOTES

Day 12

Fearless Road

Then He commissioned Joshua the son of Nun,
and said, "Be strong and courageous,
for you shall bring the sons of Israel into the land
which I swore to them,
and I will be with you."
Deuteronomy 31:23 (NASB95)

Generations before, God had promised the Israelites land rich with milk and honey that stretched from the Euphrates River to the Mediterranean Sea. With miracle after miracle, God freed them from Egyptian captivity and led them through a harsh wilderness to the border of their promised land.

But, when the Israelites considered the people already inhabiting the area, their fear overshadowed their faith in God's promise. That disobedience kept them in the wilderness for forty long years.

God commanded Joshua to lead the next generation of people into the land with strength and courage, with the promise, "I will be with you."

I confess that, like the Israelites, my fears have hindered me from immediate obedience, too. In my high school and college years, I had a

45

great fear of speaking in public. My chin trembled, my face quivered, and my heart pounded like a frenzied drummer.

In my late twenties, a group requested I pray over them before a city-wide meeting, then drafted me to speak to city leaders in the somewhat hostile gathering. I wanted to decline but God urged me to accept the nomination with the assurance He would supply the words.

With the strength and courage that could only have been from God, I accepted the assignment. The Holy Spirit quieted my fluttering heart and gave me calm, effective words to address a heated situation. Many people affirmed that my speech made a difference that night. I know they were not my words, at all. God flooded my heart with the Holy Spirit and spoke through me. He took my small act of obedience and turned it into something I could not have done on my own.

When our son deployed to a hot spot in the Middle East, fear pounded within me again, but I looked to God for help. He faithfully walked beside me through those agonizing months.

I have walked through the valley of the shadow of death. Like David in Psalm 23, I feared no evil on that treacherous path. Christ, the Good Shepherd, held me, guided me, and protected me. With Him, I had a peace that people without faith couldn't understand.

Through the years, tremendous personal losses have taken me down roads I never wanted to travel. Those times brought me to my knees before His throne—where I always found the peace and strength I needed. God remained faithful every time.

It's been my experience that obedience to God always brings rich rewards. Fear robs me of His peace.

We can be strong and courageous when He asks us to do hard things. He has a one hundred percent success rate of faithfulness to His people and His promises.

Loving Father,

Forgive me for the time I have wasted in worry and fear. Thank You for loving me, even in my doubts.

Please fill the person reading this with an extra measure of strength for the road You've asked them to travel today. May we all choose obedience to You, no matter the path before us.

In Jesus' name, amen.

Lisa Worthey Smith

 "If You Want Me To" by Ginny Owens

MY NOTES

Day 13

Caution: Men Working

He said to His disciples, "The harvest is great,
but the workers are few.
So, pray to the Lord who is in charge of the harvest;
ask Him to send more workers into His fields."
Matthew 9:37-38 (NLT)

The knock on the back door sounded throughout our nine-hundred-square-foot house. My two boys ran past me in the kitchen to get to the door. They had been waiting with great anticipation for our missionary visitors from a neighboring island to arrive. Throwing the door open, they found Betty and Matt standing on the threshold, each holding a bag of laundry in one hand and a child in the other.

I waved them in.

Betty glowed as she entered the small kitchen. "We cannot thank you enough for sponsoring us to come over for the day. Our washing machine broke, and the laundry is piling up." She eyed the bags. "Do you mind?"

"No," I assured her and pointed to the washer near the back door. "The detergent is in the cabinet. Help yourself."

Their kids deposited their shoes on the concrete patio outside and ran with my two toward the bedroom to play. Matt joined my husband in the living room at the computer.

Once she'd finished loading the machine, Betty asked if she could help me finish making lunch. When I said no, she asked if she could take a shower. She explained that most of their fresh water for bathing came from the rain barrels they had placed by the front of their house. And that she hadn't had a hot shower since the last time they were sponsored, over a month ago.

The thought of them working with the community on Ebeye, living a life of so much less, even less than my small house caused my heart to open wide. I had pictured a day of playing at the beach and enjoying good food and warm fellowship. But what these workers needed was a little help. Good food, yes, but they also needed a hot shower, a working washer and dryer, and a cool room in which to nap.

The laborers needed someone to labor alongside them, temporarily, so they could reset.

Today's verse speaks of the laborers needed to bring in the harvest. Up until I met Betty and Matt, I thought that one had to be a missionary out in the mission field to be counted as a laborer in this fashion, but sponsoring Betty and Matt and other missionaries taught me that we are all laborers for God's Kingdom. There are those who serve in other countries, and there are those who serve in their neighborhoods.

If you are part of God's Kingdom, then you are a laborer. So, be aware, God will use you—men at work, bringing in the harvest.

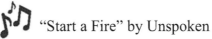

Dear Father,

I want to thank You for all those who serve in Your Kingdom to bring others into Your light. Please use me where You have me. Let me be a lover of souls, a true laborer for Your mighty Kingdom. And as Jesus instructed us, I pray You will send more workers.

In Jesus's name, amen.

Bonita Y. McCoy

♪♫ "Start a Fire" by Unspoken

MY NOTES

Day 14

Lost!

I am the light of the world.
If you follow Me, you won't be stumbling through the darkness,
because you will have the light that leads to life.

John 8:12 (NLT)

At the age of twenty-one—long before the advent of GPS and cell phones—I packed my Ford Galaxy 500 with all my belongings and drove 220 miles to a new home. My orange tabby cat occupied the passenger seat as my only traveling companion. Young, single, and carefree, I embarked on the trip without hesitation.

Folks who've known me for many years can confirm that my outlook has changed. Several frightening driving experiences through the years have eroded my once-youthful confidence. I have even declined invitations to out-of-town excursions if acceptance obligates me as the driver. However, faced with no alternative, I undertake the journey with tense shoulders and a knotted stomach.

One such trip several years ago required my daughter and me to attend a bridal tea in a large city about thirty miles from our small town. Equipped with sufficient directions, I drove the mostly-interstate miles and easily found the hostess' home in a cozy subdivision.

Day turned to evening before the celebrations ended. Darkness altered my perception of our surroundings as we set out for home. Confused, I made one wrong turn after another searching for the interstate on-ramp that would put me on the right path. We crept along, looking down one road and up another until I saw the sign looming large and welcoming approximately a block away.

"There it is!" I announced and accelerated toward the elusive highway entrance.

The long blast of a car horn behind me interrupted my sigh of gratitude. I glanced in my rear-view mirror and caught a glimpse of a vehicle crossing the intersection I'd just rolled through.

Alarm gripped my throat. "Did I run a red light?" I whispered.

"I don't know," my daughter answered and turned to look behind us. "I think so."

Shaken, I realized I had barely missed causing a terrible accident with potentially deadly results.

Darkness, disorientation, panic, and tunnel vision restricted my ability to correctly navigate that evening. I wandered in desperation, near tears at every turn that did not lead us home. I endangered our lives when I focused on what appeared to be relief from the misery rather than on the necessary steps to safely reach that goal.

And, so it is to travel through life in darkness without Jesus.

But, in Him, life has light and direction and a welcome-home destination.

John 1:4 declares of Jesus, "Life itself is in Him, and this life gives light to everyone. The light shines through the darkness, and the darkness can never extinguish it." And Jesus said of Himself, "I am the light of the world. If you follow Me, you won't be stumbling through the darkness, because you will have the light that leads to life" (John 8:12) and "I am the way, the truth, and the life" (John 14:6a).

O Giver of Life and Light,

You settle my panicking heart. You clear my disoriented thinking. You light my way with the truths of Your word. I trust all my paths to You.

In the faithful name of Jesus, amen.

Suzanne D. Nichols

♪♫ "Christ Our Hope in Life and Death"

by Keith and Kristyn Getty

MY NOTES

The Warning Signs

The Lord says,
"I will guide you along the best pathway for your life.
I will advise you and watch over you."
Psalm 32:8 (NLT)

Driving in Montreal would have been challenging for me in my Beetle. I couldn't imagine how hard it was for Oliver at the wheel of our forty-five-foot tour bus. Honking heavy traffic ... congested construction zones ... masses of pedestrians in crosswalks ... street signs with instructions in French.

We maneuvered our way toward the Ville Marie Hotel, our home for the next two nights. I had led groups through Montreal several times before, but this was Oliver's first trip to the city. So, between talking into the microphone about points of interest on our right and left, I quietly offered Oliver help with directions from my tour director seat behind him.

Just past Rue Sainte-Catherine—or Saint Catherine Street in English, Oliver took an unexpected left turn. The narrow road appeared eerily absent of vehicles. And large signs by the curbs displayed red circles with horizontal white lines across them and the words "Route Fermée."

"Uh, uh, Oliver," I stammered. "I don't remember a lot from my college French class, but I think that symbol means this road is closed."

"Let's see where it takes us," he said.

Not far ahead, we found out. Barricades prevented us from driving over the edge of a deep sinkhole in the concrete. Oliver had to back up the big bus, inch by grueling inch, guests watching through the windows, all the way to the spot where we entered.

I don't always heed God's warning signs.

If an intriguing opportunity invites me to make a left turn, sometimes I spontaneously do it. Everything about the open door may seem positive and beneficial and even Kingdom-related. Yet, I end up overcommitted and exhausted and distracted from the route God has planned for me. What if I change course too quickly and miss a sinkhole warning?

Then there's my love for travel. When I receive an email asking me to lead a tour to an exciting destination or train tour directors on a cruise ship, my initial instinct is to hit reply and type "YES, YES, YES!" Soon I find myself on the road for weeks in a row, daily wishing I could return to Sweet Home Alabama. Once again, perhaps I shoot past a warning sign by making a hasty decision.

I'm trying to slow down and better evaluate the possibilities that come my way. Instead of saying "let's see where this takes me," I'm pausing to contemplate God's advice a bit longer. His warnings can guide me as I choose a few good things to turn down and a few more good things to accept, pursue, and enjoy.

Dear God Who guides me,

I'm grateful for the wonderful things You allow me to experience in this life. Your loving directions protect me from sinkholes and steer me onto the best path—the one You have mapped out for me.

In Jesus' name I pray, amen.

Becky Alexander

♪♫ "Breathe" by Jonny Diaz

MY NOTES

Day 16

Lights on When Raining

You are the light of the world.
A city that is set on a hill cannot be hidden.
Nor do they light a lamp and put it under a basket, but on a
lampstand, and it gives light to all who are in the house.
Let your light so shine before men, that they may see your good works
and glorify your Father in heaven.
Matthew 5:14-16 (NKJV)

I usually keep my headlight switch on auto, so the headlights will automatically be on at night. But sometimes, when it's raining, it is not dark enough for them to turn on automatically. I must remember to turn them on manually when conditions are bad, so other vehicles can see me clearly.

When we experience bad conditions in our lives, we must make extra effort to shine our Christ-light so others can see Him in us. When we experience a bad day at work, a painful illness, or the death of someone close to us, we may feel like putting our light under a basket. Stress of all kinds cast a shadow over His light within us.

The apostle Paul experienced many hardships: beatings, a shipwreck, and prison. But he was always ready to share the light of the gospel with anyone he encountered. In the book of Acts, we find Paul and Silas in a prison cell with their legs in chains. *About midnight Paul and Silas were praying and singing hymns to God, and the other prisoners were listening to them. Suddenly there was such a violent earthquake that the foundations of the prison were shaken. At once all the prison doors flew open, and everyone's chains came loose.* (Acts 16: 25-26, NIV). Paul and Silas were not dwelling on their bad situation. They were rejoicing, even in prison, and look what happened!

Even amid his hardships and unjust persecution, Paul never complained. He wrote the book of Philippians from prison, yet it is filled with rejoicing. His attitude opened doors for him to share the gospel with a prison guard, and a whole family came to salvation. Regardless of his circumstances, Paul shined his Christ-light, which resulted in many people gaining eternal life.

We also need to keep our "Christ lights" on during bad conditions. It takes great faith and trust in the Lord to provide for our needs in difficult situations. Like Paul we can pray, rejoice, praise, and worship God in every circumstance. An attitude of gratitude can help us keep our lights shining. When we are feeling down, it may be hard to see the good if we keep dwelling on the bad. Let's keep our eyes focused on Jesus and our eternal destiny, and our problems in this life will seem much smaller.

Much like other drivers will see our car when the lights are on, when we shine our Christ-light during bad conditions, people notice. It may open doors for us to pour life into another person, share the gospel, and impact God's kingdom for eternity.

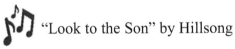

Dear Lord God,

Thank You for loving us and providing for all our needs. Thank You for making a way to share eternity with You. Help us to remember Your mercy, grace, and love even through the bad times here on earth.

In Jesus' name, amen.

Michael Loudiana, PhD

🎵 "Look to the Son" by Hillsong

MY NOTES

Day 17

 **One Way**

If you declare with your mouth, "Jesus is Lord,"
and believe in your heart that God raised him from the dead,
you will be saved.
Romans 10:9 (NIV)

My teacher aide smiled at the others in my classroom where I taught ESL, English as a Second Language, in Covington, Washington. "Just because we are on different roads doesn't mean we've gotten lost. All religions are alike. We will all wind up together." She extended her hand to the group. "The last time I went to services, the pujari explained that achieving salvation and getting to heaven is like making a day's trip to Seattle. There are many roads." My teacher aide who held to the Hindu faith stopped to take a breath. "There's the interstate and then Highway 99. You can avoid the traffic by taking a sideroad through the neighborhoods. You can ride a bike or walk. All routes take you to Seattle."

I longed to tell her about the good news of Jesus Christ—how we have eternal salvation through no works of our own but faith in Jesus. "For by grace you have been saved through faith—and this is not from yourselves, it is the gift of God—not by works, so that no one can boast" (Ephesians 2:8-9 NIV).

Although my teacher aide's spiritual leader told her there are many ways to salvation, the Bible tells us that faith in God's Son, Jesus, is the only way to heaven. "I am the Way and the Truth, and the life, no one comes to the Father except through Me." (John 14:6 NIV)

Hinduism isn't the only religion that teaches another way to Heaven. Mormon believers hold that when they die, their souls are judged. Based on their general goodness, the soul is sent to either the spirit paradise or the spirit prison. But how good is good enough? It would be scary going through life not knowing where I would end up after death.

Jehovah's Witnesses believe that only members of their group, the Jehovah Witnesses, will be saved at the end of the world, and of those, only a limited number of the most faithful will go to heaven.

The Church of Scientology believes that salvation is achieved through knowledge of self and the universe. How much knowledge do I need to receive salvation? How could I find peace without knowing how much wisdom I must have? And what about those who are born with severe mental limitations? Will they go to heaven?

The truth is there is One Way, and one way only to get to Heaven. "Salvation is found in no one else, for there is no other name under heaven given to mankind by which we must be saved" (Acts. 4:12 NIV).

"But small is the gate and narrow the road that leads to life, and only a few find it" (Matthew 7:14 NIV). Some say this teaching is narrow-minded and unfair, but I can't argue with God's word, the Bible.

There's One Way to Heaven, Christ. Won't you walk that narrow road and enter Heaven by faith in God's Son, Jesus Christ, secure in your salvation?

Lord,

Grant me opportunities to share the truth about Your Son Jesus. In Jesus' name, amen.

June Foster

♫ "Jesus is the Only Way" by Cameron Keith

MY NOTES

Day 18

Toll Road

A highway will be there,

a roadway,

and it will be called the Highway of Holiness.

The unclean will not travel on it,

but it will be for him who walks that way,

And fools will not wander on it.

No lion will be there, nor will any vicious beast go up on it;

These will not be found there.

But the redeemed will walk there.

Isaiah 35:8,9 (NASB95)

In order to pay the massive expense of building and maintaining roads and bridges, states and communities established roadblocks on their newly completed roads. Each roadblock had attendants who collected small tolls from each traveler who wanted to drive on the road. I remember keeping a few quarters in our car console in the sixties to deposit in the basket at the toll booths we encountered on our trips.

In areas with popular destinations such as Disney, toll roads are common. They lead directly to a particular venue reducing the traffic on local roadways. Of course, there is a toll to pay for that convenience. Today, tolls can cost several dollars, especially near high-traffic venues. People who travel in areas with toll roads often buy electronic long-term passes, so they don't have to stop and pay at a toll booth each time they use the roadway.

In the Scripture above, we read about the Highway of Holiness. From the verses before and after them, we learn that this highway will come at a time when we see the glory of the LORD, and the majesty of our God—when the blind will see and the deaf will hear. It will be a time of joy without sorrow or fear.

Surely a great toll would be required to travel such a road.

An enormous toll, indeed.

In the Old Testament, the sins of the people could only be covered by sprinkling the blood or ashes of animals sacrificed on an altar. Even then, the sacrifices of simple animals such as bulls and goats could not provide remission of sin, only a covering of it. The High Priest still had to go into the Holy of Holies to sprinkle blood on the Mercy Seat once a year.

Jesus, God in the flesh, came as our sinless and blameless High Priest and offered Himself as a one-time sacrifice to pay for all my sins and yours. Only His blood could cleanse us from our unrighteousness. His permanent "toll paid" gift to travel the Highway of Holiness came at a high cost to Him, but He gives it freely to us. We only have to accept it.

He mentioned it from the cross when He said "It is finished."

Tetelestai in the Greek, meaning the debt is paid in full.

Dear Father,

Thank You for providing a way for us to walk on the road of the redeemed. I could never travel there if Jesus had not paid the price for me. Thank You for loving me.

As I walk the path You have for me today, give me opportunities to share about the tremendous gift You provided.

In Jesus' name, amen.

Lisa Worthey Smith

 "He Paid it All" by Brandon Heath

MY NOTES

Slow – Blind Turn Ahead

Lord had said to Abram,
"Leave your native country, your relatives,
and your father's family, and go to a land that I will show you."
… So Abram departed as the Lord had instructed,
and Lot went with him.
Genesis 12:1&4 (NLT)

The engines of the plane hummed as the landing gear released beneath us. My husband and I had spent the last two months packing our belongings to move to a tiny island in the Pacific for a job opportunity. Neither of us had ever been there, but a little research led us to believe it was a slice of paradise on Earth.

My heart raced as I peeked out the window trying to catch my first glimpse of our new home. We'd left everything we'd ever known including our family and friends to go on this adventure, sure that God was in it.

As I leaned across the armrest, the plane tilted on its side, and I saw below me a crescent-shaped piece of land. The words small and isolated popped into my mind. The plane straightened, and as we descended, all I could see around me was crisp, blue water.

We were going in blind.

I couldn't see the land. I had to trust that the pilot knew what he was doing. When the engines revved and I heard the screeching of the wheels on the tarmac, I let out a breath I hadn't realized I'd been holding.

Now came the hard part—trusting God in this new unknown life we were about to enter.

Abram's story reminds me of God's call on our lives. Many times, God asks for our obedience without a lot of detailed instructions. He wants us to trust that He will show us the way as He did for Abram and his family. He wants us to follow Him even when we can't see what's around the turn or under the plane.

Abram obeyed without question. He packed up his household, his livestock, and the people who worked for him and headed off to the land of Canaan, not sure what to expect. But he had one thing he could count on—God's promise to bless him.

My husband and I never regretted our time on the island. It was one of our favorite adventures. And like Abram, God blessed us because of our obedience to go. We made lifelong friends, reaped great gain and experience, and confirmed that regardless of culture, everyone needs our Savior.

If God calls you to make a change, big or little, listen to His voice. He won't fail you, He won't leave you, and you won't regret it.

Father,

May I trust in You wholeheartedly, and when I doubt, let me recall all Your promises to me in Your Word. Fill my heart with Your courage and place within me a heart of obedience.

In Jesus' name, amen.

Bonita Y. McCoy

🎵 "Spirit Lead Me" by Hillsong

MY NOTES

Day 20

Roundabout

Show me Your ways, O Lord, teach me Your paths.
Psalm 25:4 (NIV)

The sunny day beckoned us to enjoy a few hours in a town my husband and I have watched evolve through the years. With each visit, we lament the loss of history replaced by new developments.

Traffic management can be a maddening challenge for an area with increasing numbers of businesses and residents relying on the roadways. However, off the main paths, this city has installed a method of navigating an intersection called a roundabout. Its circular design forces drivers to slow down but not stop. Vehicles travel in the same direction rather than crossing paths as in a traditional four-way or two-way stop. Traffic flows in a sort of choreographed waltz.

Although roundabouts have been popular in Europe for decades, their introduction in America during the first half of the twentieth century found resistance due to flaws in the earliest configurations. Difficulties understanding the movement and merges led to horns blaring, drivers shouting, and many accidents. Even after improvements, the oddity continues to cause intimidation and alarm.

My husband turned off the main road in search of a lesser-congested path for our wanderings. Along the way, we discovered a roundabout. Faced with no choice but to follow the curve to our desired exit point, my husband smoothly adjusted to the rhythm of the dance, and we came out of the circle unscathed.

~~~

As Joshua prepared to lead the Israelites to conquer the Promised Land, the people camped for fourteen days at Gilgal on the Jericho plains. They celebrated Passover there and waited to know the Lord's battle plan for their first conquest in the new land.

Jericho's residents knew of the mighty victories God had given Israel. Watchmen on the city's wall witnessed the crossing of the Jordan River on dry ground during flood stage. Assuming the Israelites planned to attack, Jericho's terrified inhabitants sheltered within the protection of their great walled city.

But Israel did not attack. Instead, they followed God's strange-sounding instructions.

Protected by armed guards at the front and rear, seven priests with rams' horns formed a line. Priests carrying the Ark of the Covenant followed. The people were instructed to be silent as the ram's horns sounded a continual tone. The troupe marched around Jericho in this manner once each day for six days, then returned to camp.

On the seventh day, the odd processional marched again, completing the circuit seven times.

At the final turn, the priests signaled with a long blast on the rams' horns and Joshua gave the command, "Shout! For the Lord has given you the city!"

The people shouted as the horns blared. The walls of Jericho collapsed and the army charged straight in to capture the city.

Joshua chapter six records God's miraculous use of a circle, a sight more intimidating than a roundabout, with an outcome more rewarding than safely reaching the exit lane. The shouts and blasting of horns around Jericho signaled victory, not failure; and praise of a mighty God, not alarm in a circle of uncertainty.

O Faithful God,

When the challenges of the day bring confusion or anxiety, help me trust You to guide me through.

In the victorious name of Jesus, I pray, amen.

Suzanne D. Nichols

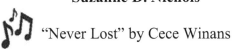 "Never Lost" by Cece Winans

MY NOTES

Day 21

Shoulder Drop-off

Submit yourselves, then, to God.
Resist the devil, and he will flee from you.
James 4:7 (NIV)

I thought we were going to die. My ten-year-old self sat in the back seat of my parents' car, looking out the window. The car kept getting closer and closer to the brink. I thought we would fall a mile if the tires slipped. All I could see was farmland down below, and I could no longer see the edge of the road.

We finished exploring Yosemite National Park, and my dad had the bright idea to take a shortcut and leave the park via Tioga Pass. My dad's shortcuts were legendary, but this one was the most terrifying by far. All I remember was a single-lane road with a cliff face on the left and a long steep fall on the right, with no barrier.

We were at the top of the pass and could see there was no traffic coming up from the bottom, so my dad started down. About halfway down we went around a curve and saw a truck approaching. My dad inched his way towards the drop-off so the truck could get by us.

Eventually, we passed by the truck and made our way to the bottom, but I never wanted to be that close to the edge of a long plunge again.

Many of us experience a shoulder drop-off in our spiritual lives when we are tempted. We want to know where the line is, so we can get as close to it as possible without going over. Some of us may be so close that our tires are dangling over the edge.

This happened to King David, and he succumbed to temptation. David was walking around the palace roof when he spotted Bathsheba bathing on the roof of her house. Rooftop bathing was a common practice in Jerusalem during that time. So, what was David doing on his palace roof looking at other rooftops? And once he spotted Bathsheba, why didn't he look away? You may remember that David had her brought to him and had her husband killed. David fell over the edge, and he fell long and hard.

God's word does not tell us to identify the line between temptation and sin and see how close we can get. Instead, it says to *flee from sexual immorality* (1 Corinthians 6:18), *flee from idolatry* (1 Corinthians 10:14), *flee from the love of money* (1 Timothy 6:11), and *flee from the evil desires of youth* (2 Timothy 2:22).

The devil works hard to determine the most effective temptation for each of us. This nice, shiny temptation may lure us right up to the

82

shoulder drop-off, and before we know it, we are over the edge. But the Bible also says, "Resist the devil, and he will flee from you." God will never let us be tempted beyond what we can resist, but at the first sign, we should submit ourselves to God and run away from that shoulder drop-off as fast as we can.

Dear Lord God,

Thank You for Your mercy, grace, and forgiveness. Help us recognize temptation and resist it, so the devil will flee from us.

In Jesus' name, amen.

Michael Loudiana, PhD

 "Yield Not to Temptation" Al Green

MY NOTES

Day 22

Road Closed

So do not fear, for I am with you; do not be dismayed,
for I am your God. I will strengthen you and help you.
I will uphold you with my righteous right hand.
Isaiah 41:10 (NIV)

My husband backed our thirty-six-foot Class A Tiffin into the parking spot with his usual, astute skill. Five months in balmy Harlingen, Texas, nestled in the lower Rio Grande Valley thirty miles from the Mexican border sounded wonderful. No snow, sleet, or icy roads.

Living and traveling in our RV full time allowed us visits to many of the national parks, presidents' home places, and the Lewis and Clark trails. We wanted to remain on the road for another five years before settling down.

We spent the winter of 2019 with one adventure after another from the zoo in Brownsville, Texas, to short trips into Mexico by way of the small border town of Progreso to frequenting the authentic Mexican restaurants in the area. We celebrated Christmas with the wonderful people staying in the park. New Year's Day transitioned us to a new, wonderful year living the life we'd always imagined.

But in March 2020, everything changed. News on the internet and TV spoke of a strange, new virus coming to the United States from China. Scientists were caught off-guard with no antivirals to combat its spread. The virus swept through our country like a tsunami.

COVID-19 had become a pandemic. The entire world was at the mercy of a disease.

My husband and I had plans. We weren't getting any younger and time was running out. Yet we'd encountered a huge, blaring sign that warned: Road Closed. The road we'd planned to travel had shut tight.

We prayed and felt the Lord leading us home to Alabama but with no banjo on our knees. We left Harlingen one afternoon and headed toward Cullman. Three days later, we secured a spot in the local RV park.

Three years have passed now, and the disease isn't as rampant as in the early days. Masks are no longer mandatory, and I can go to the salon for a haircut. God provided. We were able to purchase a home during the worst of the months with a lower interest rate than what is available today.

Looking back on those times, I've come to some realizations. God was so good to us. Not once did I fear the disease. God knows the day I was born and the day He'll take me home. I trusted God, and if He chose for me to leave this earth after a bout with Covid, that was okay because I knew Heaven awaited. The peace of God reigned in our home and hearts the entire time. Though we hit one of life's roadblocks, God turned us around and set us onto the road where He wanted us.

The sovereign God's ways are perfect. Though we don't completely understand, we can fully trust Him.

Dear Lord,

We worship You, the God who knows all things. You possess all wisdom and all power. We never have to fear no matter what happens in our lives. Thank You, mighty God, for making a way for us when we hit a closed road. In the name of Jesus, amen.

June Foster

♫ "I Will Not Fear" by Chris McQuisition

MY NOTES

Day 23

No U-Turn

The LORD was going before them
in a pillar of cloud by day to lead them on the way,
and in a pillar of fire by night to give them light,
that they might travel by day and by night.
Exodus 13:21 (NASB95)

Many rural roads are littered with flattened squirrels who second-guessed their route. I've watched them wait for a clearing in traffic and dart into the road. However, in the middle of the road, they see cars coming. Tails flitting, they spin around calculating the squirrel math and choose to go to the other side of the road. By then—you guessed it—cars are headed toward them from the other direction.

Equally panicked for them, I've tried to direct them by cheering and motioning from inside my car. "Keep going. Hurry. Don't go back. You can do it."

Regardless of my encouragement, sometimes by the time they finished their calculations, they lost all bravery and made poor decisions. They saw the danger in front of them, and a greater mortal danger behind them and were overcome with terror. I gave them the correct solution, but they didn't always listen.

In the Exodus Scripture passage above, the LORD had told His people He would lead them into a land flowing with milk and honey. He protected His people while plagues befell their captors. When they left Egypt, God provided a pillar of cloud by day and a pillar of fire by night for them to follow, a visible road sign, to direct them.

With an angry army pursuing them, God led the Israelites to camp at the edge of the Red Sea. Impossibly trapped between a sea of water and an army sent to kill them, like squirrels in the middle of the road, their human equations seemed to equal death either way. They cried that they should have gone back and languished under slavery rather than die from Pharaoh's spear.

In response to their trepidation, the LORD told Moses, "Why are you crying out to Me? Tell the sons of Israel to go forward."

God parted the sea and His people crossed "the midst of the sea on dry land." He also continued to provide them the pillar of cloud by day and the pillar of fire by night, during their journey. They looked at their situation through human eyes and they doubted Him. He knew their path would lead them into danger, but those dangers would be opportunities for Him to show His great love and care for them.

God has laid out a path for us. At times we will encounter difficulties and be tempted to turn around, but He will light each step of the way for us to move forward when we look to Him for direction.

Father in heaven,

Forgive me when I allow fear to freeze me or make me look back. Help me to focus on You, what You've called me to do, and what lies ahead so I will not waver in doubt of the direction or timing You have for me.

Thank You for loving me and giving me Your Word to guide me along the way. Keep me moving forward to Your goal.

In Jesus name, amen.

Lisa Worthey Smith

 "Tell Your Heart to Beat Again" by Danny Gokey

MY NOTES

Day 24

Do Not Enter

Enter through the narrow gate.
For wide is the gate and broad and easy to travel is the path
that leads the way to destruction and eternal loss,
and there are many who enter through it.
Matthew 7:13 (Amplified Bible)

When my husband and I travel in our RV, we look for wide-open roads that can accommodate our rig. The bigger the highway, the more room we'll have to maneuver around other vehicles without putting anyone in danger, especially semis or other RVs.

On one trip in July, we headed to a well-known campground to stop for a few days. The campground offered activities for our boys including a play area and a pool. We made great time, but as we neared the end of the trip, the GPS sent us down a thin, narrow road. The farther we went the narrower the road became.

Then the calm voice on the device directed us to take a right turn onto a path no wider than a walking trail. Jamming the gear shift into park, my husband pulled out his phone and called the campground.

Sure enough, the facility had a back entrance that hadn't been used in years, and our GPS had led us down the wrong path trying in vain to get us to our destination.

In today's Scripture, we are warned about taking the wrong path. Unlike the road my husband and I encountered in our RV, God instructs us to choose the narrow road.

Too often, we watch as people we love choose the easy, wide road. They pick this road for many reasons. Sometimes, it's simpler and doesn't cost them anything like a friendship or a change in lifestyle. Sometimes, they are following someone else's example who isn't living a godly life, and sometimes, it's because they have never heard of our Jesus.

The narrow road looks to them too hard to maneuver and too restrictive, like that walking trail looked to me and my husband.

But as Christians, we know better. The narrow road may be less traveled and at times difficult, but with Jesus, all things are possible. We know the narrow way holds blessings, a relationship with our Father, and a deep inner healing that can only come from being grafted into the vine.

Our job is to act as the Do Not Enter sign for those who are headed down the wide road. Proverbs 24:11-12 tells us *Rescue those being led away to death; hold back those staggering toward slaughter. If you say, "But we knew nothing about this," does not he who weighs the heart perceive it?*

We are the sign that says Do Not Enter and the one that points to the One Way.

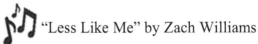

Father,

Open my heart, so I may be a Sower of the Truth. Let me be that sign pointing others to You and Your Son, Jesus. For He alone is the way and salvation comes through no other name. Make me bold, make me courageous, make me more like Jesus.

In Jesus' name, amen.

Bonita Y. McCoy

🎵 "Less Like Me" by Zach Williams

MY NOTES

Day 25

Rest Area

...and together they set out

from Ur of the Chaldeans to go to Canaan.

But when they came to Haran, they settled there.

Genesis 11:31b (NIV)

Interstate rest areas provide travelers with pleasant stopping places and can serve to fulfill a variety of needs. Staffed and maintained by the Highway Department, the facilities are clean, safe, easily accessible, and situated in welcoming surroundings.

My husband and I look for these rest areas wherever we travel. We stretch our legs, breathe a bit of fresh air, visit the restrooms, and occasionally peruse the maps on display inside the building. If we need a meal or a stimulating cup of coffee along the way, a fast-food restaurant provides a different type of refreshment and brief respite.

We don't linger. We don't have a dog to walk or young children who need to run off some pent-up energy. However, these stops do provide temporary relief for our road-weary minds and bodies.

As welcome as these breaks are, the trip must continue if we are to reach our intended destination. How incomplete and unfulfilling would our journey be if we stayed at a rest stop or restaurant for

97

months or years? Aside from facing charges of loitering, we would be disappointed and discontented with such a decision.

Genesis 11:27-32 records the incomplete travel plans of the clan of Terah. Following the Great Flood, the descendants of Shem, one of Noah's three sons, settled in an area about 600 miles south of Mount Ararat known then as Chaldea or Babylonia. Generations later, Shem's descendant, Terah, gathered his son, Abram, Abram's wife Sarai, and his grandson, Lot, and left his home in Ur of the Chaldeans. The small caravan headed north along the Euphrates River.

We learn from Genesis 11:31, their destination was Canaan, a vast and beautiful area bordering the Mediterranean Sea. However, within 400 miles of their goal, they stopped—and lingered—in Haran.

Terah settled in Haran and prospered there. His plans to take his family to Canaan faded with the passing years. He died in Haran, never having experienced the joy of reaching his projected journey's end.

Haran became more than a rest area. Terah stopped short of his intended destination and Haran became good enough.

Following Terah's death, God called Abram to leave Haran and *"go to the land I will show you."* Without knowing where God would lead, Abram obeyed. As he packed his possessions, perhaps he recalled his father's unrealized plans to go to Canaan. Perhaps the prospects that pressed Terah to leave Ur rekindled anew in Abram. He pointed his caravan toward Canaan not yet knowing if this was God's plan.

God did, indeed, lead Abram to Canaan. He revealed His promise at Shechem saying, "*To your descendants I will give this land.*"

As a follower of Christ, I have a calling to come out of Babylon, to leave Ur behind, and to guide my descendants toward God's unique blessings for their futures. The journey is long and difficult and I'm tempted to linger at the rest area. But I must turn my caravan toward Canaan in expectation of God's faithfulness to fulfill His promises.

O God of Precious Promises,

Draw me close to hear Your voice. Spur me when I need to move. Give me faith to know You go before me. Guide me as I lead others in Your way.

I pray in Jesus' name, amen.

Suzanne D. Nichols

 "Find Us Faithful" by Steve Green

MY NOTES

Day 26

Caution – Danger Ahead

Put on the full armor of God,
so that you can take your stand against the devil's schemes.
Ephesians 6:11 (NIV)

It was one of those Sundays. Why did those pesky frustrations seem to fall on the Lord's Day? Yet, not only on the first day of the week but other days as well. They came more frequently than I wanted to admit.

I stood at my bathroom mirror, attempting to coerce my hair into the style I wanted. No success.

"June, have you seen my new shirt?" my husband called from the closet as he dressed for church.

If he'd only keep his shirts organized by colors like I showed him, he'd be able to find them when he got dressed. "I arranged your shirts last week. If you can't keep them that way, I'm sorry." Immediately I regretted my sharp tone but continued the battle with my hair.

Finally in the car, we headed toward church. At a four-way stop, Joe slammed on the brakes to avoid a car that'd run the stop sign. I breathed out a sigh of relief. "Thank you, Lord, for saving us from a near collision."

"Whew, that was close. That guy wasn't even looking." Joe shook his head in frustration.

We sat to hear words of wisdom from our pastor, but my mind wandered like a hiker in the woods who strayed from the trail. At lunch, when my husband asked about my favorite part of the sermon, I had no answer.

At home, I plopped down on the couch and picked up my Bible. A caution flag arose in my mind. Today was one of those days I especially needed to don my spiritual armor, and I'd forgotten.

Some days when I get dressed, I need to put on different clothes besides my usual jeans and T-shirt. In the Bible, these spiritual garments are called the armor of God. The Bible describes each part of the armor we need in Ephesians 6, verse 14.

Daily, I buckle the belt of truth around my waist which gives me a little squeeze when I'm tempted to exaggerate, tell a little white fib, or blatantly lie.

I go to my closet, find my breastplate, and slip it on. Each time the contraption shifts, I'm reminded the Lord has declared me His righteous one.

I strap the gospel of peace on my feet, prepared to stand firm and ready to work.

Before I go out the door, I pick up my shield with which I can protect myself from any attacks of the devil or his minions.

As I leave the house, I look in the mirror and put on my helmet of salvation which constantly reminds me to Whom I belong.

I will not forget my weapon of choice, the sword of the Spirit which is the Word of God. Some of the words are in my head, but if my memory fails me, I can check my Bible to find others.

Caution. Don't leave home without your spiritual clothes.

Dear Lord,

Thank You for providing Your spiritual armor to protect me.

In Jesus' name, amen.

June Foster

♪♫ "Head to Toe" by Christy Nockels

MY NOTES

Day 27

Yield

Jesus called them together and said,
"You know that the rulers of the Gentiles lord it over them, and their
high officials exercise authority over them. Not so with you. Instead,
whoever wants to become great among you must be your servant, and
whoever wants to be first must be your slave."
Matthew 20:25 - 27 (NIV)

I think of myself as a courteous driver. I will often let a car merge in front of me when they are in the lane with the dreaded Yield sign. I get irritated when I am in the yield lane and car after car goes by without allowing me enough room to safely merge with traffic. Don't they owe me, since I would do the same for them?

Our culture values fairness. But the Kingdom of God is countercultural. Being great in God's kingdom is about submitting oneself for the sake of God's glory and for the benefit of others.

Being a well-organized introvert, I keep a running list of things to do in my head. Sometimes, I may obsess over this list and miss out on an opportunity to serve others unless God brings it to my attention.

This may be what happened to Moses as he tended his father-in-law's flock.

Moses had fled from Egypt and knew of God's promise to deliver the Hebrews from slavery in Egypt. Moses probably thought that this deliverance would have nothing to do with him. After all, how could a simple shepherd do anything about this? He was likely thinking about his shepherding to-do list when he saw a bush aflame yet not consumed.

As he approached the burning bush, God spoke to him and said, "Go. I am sending you to Pharaoh to bring my people the Israelites out of Egypt."

Moses answered, "Who am I that I should go to Pharaoh and bring the Israelites out of Egypt?" Like many of us, Moses could not see how God could use him to do such a great thing. He was not ready to yield to God.

But God was patient with Moses. He gave Moses detailed instructions about what to say, what miracles to show the Egyptians, and how they would leave with Egyptian plunder.

But Moses still balked, "Pardon your servant, Lord. I have never been eloquent. I am slow of speech and tongue." The introverted side of me can relate to Moses. I can understand his fear of public speaking and his resistance.

Finally, after God provided Moses' brother Aaron as a helper, Moses yielded and returned to Egypt to deliver the people of Israel. The rest of the story can be found in the book of Exodus; the plagues in Egypt, the first Passover, the escape across the Red Sea, and arriving at the promised land.

When God shows me an opportunity to do something great for His kingdom, like writing, often I will think that I cannot do this thing by myself. Then I remember that the creator of the universe will be working with me, and I don't need to do it all by myself. I just need to yield.

Dear Lord God,

Thank You for the opportunity to serve You and others. Help me to have eyes to see, ears to hear, and a servant's heart, knowing that You will always be with me.

In Jesus' name, amen.

Michael Loudiana, PhD

 "Available" by Elevation Worship

MY NOTES

No Rest Stops

"For when the foolish took their lamps, they took no oil with them,
but the prudent took oil in flasks along with their lamps."
"Be on the alert then, for you do not know the day nor the hour.
Matthew 25:3,4, 13 (NASB95)

I'm a packer, planner, and preparer by nature. Along with the necessities, I pack plenty of "What if?" extras. I have napkins, a first aid kit, and snacks in the front seat, and behind us are extra bottles of water in a small cooler ready for dry throats. Our luggage includes plenty of clothing items for different temperatures along with raingear, extra shoes, and sweaters—just in case.

My equally prudent husband checks the tires, wiper blades, and fluid levels prior to a trip. While traveling, he watches the gas gauge and refuels when the needle nears the half-empty mark.

If you live in or have traveled through Utah, you might be familiar with Interstate 70 which includes the longest stretch—110 miles—of road in the US with no gas stations, bathrooms, or exits. The scenery is a fantastic blend of spruce and jack pine forests, bogs, rocks, and low-lying hills. "What if?" tingles along the back of my neck when I think about traveling over 100 miles of desolation.

Signs warn travelers about the barren road ahead so drivers can estimate their time and plan accordingly. The women in the Scripture reference above didn't have such a specific timeline. They had all been invited to attend a wedding and only had to wait on the way from the groom's house to the bride's home. As soon as the father of the groom approved—the groom would come to get the bride and everyone could begin the celebration.

While they waited, the women became drowsy and fell asleep. Five of the ten women prepared for the delay by bringing extra oil for their lamps. The remaining five did not. When the groom came for his bride, half of the group was prepared. The other half thought they had time to get more oil, but didn't, and could not attend the feast.

Precious friends, we know our groom, Jesus, is coming for His bride, those He loves and who love Him—the church. We know the hour of His coming grows closer with every passing day. While we wait for Christ to return it's easy to look to the immediate needs of family, occupations, and other responsibilities, instead of our mission. Jesus told us to go and share the good news with everyone. He said we should minister to the weak and needy and show His love to others so they will come to know Him, too.

We don't know how much time we have left until we meet Him face to face. It's easy to become sleepy while we wait and drift into thoughts of things that only matter here on earth instead of things that will have an eternal impact for His kingdom. Let's use that time wisely to point others to the urgency of their decisions so they will be ready for the groom who will usher us into the greatest celebration of all.

Dear Father,

Forgive me when I behave like those who were only prepared for a temporary wait.

The signs are abundant that You will return shortly. Help me see opportunities to share that good news today and every day until You come.

In Jesus' name, amen.

Lisa Worthey Smith

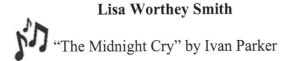 "The Midnight Cry" by Ivan Parker

MY NOTES

Day 29

Detour

When Pharaoh finally let the people go,
God did not lead them along the main road
that runs through Philistine territory,
even though that was the shortest route to the Promise Land ...
So God led them in a roundabout way through the wilderness
toward the Red Sea.
Exodus 13:17-18 (NLT)

Recently, my husband and I experienced one of God's detours.

Cancer. The call came one Tuesday evening in February informing us

of the diagnosis and the appointments for him over the next two days

to see a surgeon and an oncologist.

The mere mention of the word has the power to turn you in a

different direction. Plans change. Travel stops. Life slows to what is

necessary and what can be managed.

One son returned home to help with our five-acre hobby farm,

and family came in droves over the months to visit, since we couldn't

go to them.

Our church friends prayed, ministered, and encouraged us. They

helped us to focus on God's love instead of the situation.

When God led the Israelites out of Egypt through Moses, He didn't take them along the direct route to the Promised Land. No, He sent them on a detour.

God knew leading them through the Philistine territory would result in a battle, and He also knew the Israelites didn't have the heart for a fight—they'd turn and flee back to Egypt at the first sign of trouble.

Interesting how God works. He often sends us on detours, not to make our lives harder, but because our hearts aren't ready for what lies ahead.

Like the Israelites and their tendency to turn back, it's easy for me to think about the days before the cancer. I long for the time when I could make plans and see them through without a hitch. But I dare not go backward. I must press forward through this time of detour.

In Exodus, God sent the Israelites on a detour, but He did not leave them there alone. He went before them as a pillar of cloud during the day and as a pillar of fire at night. Giving Moses directions, He had them camp between Migdol and along the shore of the Red Sea. God wanted Pharoah to think that they were confused and trapped.

But God had a plan to show His people and the Egyptians His glory and power. Their detour led to the spectacular parting of the Red Sea and the following destruction of their enemy.

I know this detour God set us on has honed my faith and the faith of my husband, who had to walk the harder part. When it looked as if we were trapped by circumstances or confused by the outcome, God's glory shone even brighter.

A friend with the needed information, an appointment available at the right time, and help showing up just as it was necessary were all rays of God's glory shining forth, promising His presence with us along the way.

Detours bring difficulties, but God never steers us the wrong way. Perhaps He has sent you a detour, if so, take it. The shortest route is not always the one that leads to the greatest outcome.

Dear Father,

Bless me on Your detours. May the long way produce in me a desire to lean even closer to You. And may I reflect Your glory, Your power, and Your presence in my life. In Jesus' name, amen.

Bonita Y. McCoy

 "The Blessing" Kari Jobe with Elevation Worship

MY NOTES

Day 30

Temporary Lane Closure

In his heart, a man plans his course,
but the Lord determines his steps.
Proverbs 16:9 (NIV)

Designs for a much-needed home renovation lay neatly tucked into my sketch pad. My husband's timeline for completion, including his plan of action, headlined page one in the pad lying closed on my desk at home.

Writing projects, I'd planned to devote a large block of time completing, remained sidelined in my computer.

I shoved these images to the back of my mind as I sat four feet from my mother's side and 250 miles from the work I'd left behind.

I didn't mind the interruption, only that it was unexpected. My husband Roger and I were glad retirement freed us to attend to my mother's needs. But we began the eleven-week venture unaware of the time and attention it would require. My mother's health had declined more than I'd realized.

Roger and I worked as a team. He provided the muscle where I couldn't manage and the supplemental physical therapy exercises my mother needed. While I stayed with my mom day and night, his arrival each morning brought balm to my soul. He was my rock as well as my soft place to fall.

Before long, he became the errand runner, grocery shopper, laundry man, and chauffeur to doctor's appointments. Still, most days lacked the activity he craved. To pass the time, he downloaded movies to his phone, walked outdoors, took a nap or two each day, and became a fan of the HG channel. He even bought a guitar on the local Facebook Marketplace so he could work on his fledgling skills.

About three weeks into our stay, he returned from an errand and asked me to walk outside with him. He spoke softly as we ambled through a carpet of rusty-red and yellow maple leaves.

"Before I left earlier, I sat in the car lamenting over the projects piling up at home. Then God spoke into my spirit, 'You're looking at this all wrong. Why did I create you and place you in this world? Was it not so you could find Me and help others find Me? These things you are so concerned about—that work left unfinished; those accomplishments unattained—won't matter for eternity. I've placed you here, in this situation, at this time, for a reason and I am able to make you fruitful where I have planted you.'"

I clutched his hand and wept, enveloped in the comforting reality of God's sovereignty, and overwhelmed by His loving kindness toward us. His correction is good and profitable for our health and safety. His guidance leads us in the right paths even when we don't understand His movements.

Those weeks with my mother revealed countless hidden blessings. I witnessed the care and concern of friends, neighbors, and relatives. I learned to release control, realizing I can't do everything. I found I could adjust my expectations without jeopardizing my goals. I gained a deeper gratitude for a husband who so generously lived out his love and commitment to me. And I saw his fruitfulness multiply as he gave of his wisdom, knowledge, energy, and skills to meet the needs of others.

O Sovereign Lord,

I give You control of my expectations, my well-thought-out plans and goals, and even my unmet hopes. Let me face each day at peace in the center of where You've placed me.

In Jesus' name I pray, amen.

Suzanne D. Nichols

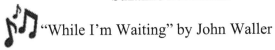 "While I'm Waiting" by John Waller

MY NOTES

Day 31

Are We There, Yet?

Brethren, I do not regard myself as having laid hold of it yet;
but one thing I do:
forgetting what lies behind and reaching forward to what lies ahead,
I press on toward the goal
for the prize of the upward call of God in Christ Jesus.
Philippians 3:13,14 (NASB95)

"Mom. Are we there yet?" Our son inquired from the backseat of our packed minivan.

"Almost." I put my pointer finger near my thumb to give him a visual representation of how near we were to our vacation destination.

He squirmed in the car seat and let out an extra loud sigh. "Can we stop and get a hamburger?"

"We just ate, honey. I know you're tired of sitting, but we'll be at the hotel soon. Then we can eat and get started with our beach fun."

He pointed to a fast-food restaurant billboard that displayed a hamburger dripping with cheese. Crispy fries and a milkshake added to the sign's mouth-watering temptation. "But, Mom…" A few miles later, a sign boasting about a steaming hot pizza incited a request for another stop. Disappointment about all the deliciousness we left behind rang in his voice and in his forlorn little face as we passed by such a tasty opportunity.

After another hour, I told him, "Okay, sweetie. Put on your shoes. We're almost there."

His demeanor shifted to excitement. He reached for his Velcro sneakers and tugged them on while he listed all the things he wanted to do once we arrived. Changing his focus to the destination eliminated his discontent about what he missed along the way.

As Christians, many things in the present try to steer us away from the future God has for us. The world is filled with billboard-sized temptations promising something wonderful, that usually provide immediate, though temporary, satisfaction. Once we veer from God's path, the more blind we become to the falsehoods the temptations display.

Waiting for God to answer longstanding prayers amid pain and suffering can bring us to a deeper faith in God. However, without complete focus on Him, the enemy can use those times to magnify the pain and deceive us into blaming God for it. If we succumb to that deception, we can be distracted to the point of despair. There, the enemy tells us we should give up and take a different route with immediate gratification instead of trusting Almighty God.

We're all traveling on a journey of faith. Our finish line awaits beyond the hairpin curves, steep mountains, and tempting distractions. The choices we make each day either guide us toward God or lead us away from Him and our ultimate goal. Together, let's press forward toward our true goal, our calling, no matter how beguiling the temptation to give up or take a different path. I'm cheering for you!

Dear Father in Heaven,

Thank You for providing Your Word, a roadmap leading us to the finish line in heaven, and the magnificent prize of being Yours for eternity.

Be with us today as we navigate our world filled with suffering, lies, and temptations. May our eyes always be focused on You rather than the temporary things of the world. Give us the determination and stamina to keep going when the final destination isn't yet in sight.

I pray in Jesus' name, amen.

Lisa Worthey Smith

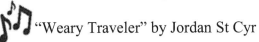 "Weary Traveler" by Jordan St Cyr

MY NOTES

About
the Authors

Becky Alexander is literally "on the road" six months of the year. She works as a tour director, leading groups throughout the U.S. and Canada. Currently, she is on assignment with Road Scholar in the Southeast—Charleston, Savannah, Jekyll Island, St. Augustine, and Nashville.

As a devotional writer for Guideposts, Becky's work appears in *Mornings with Jesus*, *Pray a Word a Day*, and other publications. "Connected by Kindness" in *Chicken Soup for the Soul: Miracles & Divine Intervention* received first-place awards from Carolina Christian Writers Conference and Southern Christian Writers Conference.

Becky collaborated with her biologist brother and teacher sister to write *Clover's Wildflower Field Trip*. The award-winning children's book is filled with scientific facts and vocabulary words that support elementary STEM standards. Now, she's working on *Clover and Critters in the Creek*.

Connect with Becky:

Send a happy message and find all of her happy books at

www.happychairbooks.com.

Learn about Becky's life with a prosthetic left arm at

www.onesmileonearm.com.

An award-winning author, **June Foster** is a retired teacher with a BA in Education and a MA in counseling. June began writing Christian romance in 2010 as she and her husband traveled the US in their RV. Her adventures provide a rich source of information for her novels. She brags about visiting a location before it becomes the setting in her next book.

To date, June has written over thirty contemporary romance and romantic suspense novels and novellas. June uses her training in counseling and her Christian beliefs in creating characters who encounter real-life difficulties yet live victorious lives. She's published with Winged Publications.

June is active in her church and her ladies' fellowship group. She enjoys writing devotionals as well as fiction. She frequently attends writers' conferences such as Blue Lake Writers' Conference and Florida Christian Writers Conference.

Her novel, *The Inn at Cranberry Cove,* won the 2021 Selah award for Romantic Suspense. It is available on Amazon in paperback, hardback, and eBook format. In 2023, June won the Ames Award for her book *Christmas at Cranberry Cove*, book three in the same series.

 Visit June at www.junefoster.com or scan the QR code to the left to view a complete list of her books.

Also, visit her Amazon page for all her latest  books.

 **Michael Loudiana, PhD** is a physicist with a distinguished 35-year career in research and systems engineering supporting American missile defense systems. During his career he achieved status as a Boeing Technical Fellow, was awarded three US patents, and published dozens of professional articles.

Since retiring, Mike has completed classes on Christian ministry and leadership at Highlands College, and classes on creation science at Answers in Genesis and Creation Ministries International. He is currently a church small group leader, speaker, and technical reviewer for the Journal of Creation.

Dr Loudiana is also working on his first book about science and the Bible. Through writing devotionals for *Coffee with God, volume 3,* Mike discovered the joy of composing material that contrasted sharply from the technical and professional style required of his career.

Mike grew up in Spokane, Washington and has five children and six grandchildren in the Seattle area. He lives in Alabama with his wife, Phyllis. Mike and Phyllis love to travel. Phyllis loves to cook and quilt and Dr. Loudiana loves to eat and spend time at the computer

writing, coding, and performing data analysis.

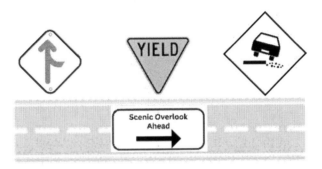

Bonita Y. McCoy hails from the Great State of Alabama where she lives on a five-acre farm with two dogs, two cows, one cat, and one husband who she's had since circa 1989.

She is a mother to three grown sons who have all flown the coop.

Her background includes a degree in Journalism from Mississippi State University as well as ten years teaching high school literature and writing classes to some of the best students, ever. She also served for twelve years as the Research Paper Coordinator for Life Christian Academy.

Her publishing adventure started at the ripe old age of thirteen when she worked for two years as a staff reporter for her school newspaper, *The Bearcat Chatter*. Her senior year she worked on the School Yearbook as Junior Section Editor and did ad layouts for *The Gulfport Star*, a local newspaper.

More recent adventures include publishing her *Amy Kate Cozy Mystery* series through Winged Publications and being a finalist in both the Selah Awards and Silver Falchion Awards with that series.

Along with other members of Word Weavers of North Alabama, she contributes to the *COFFEE with God* series of devotional books (Kerysso Press). Of the three published to date, one volume was a Selah Award finalist and several devotions in other volumes have won individual awards, which helps spread His Word even further.

She loves God, and she loves to write. Her blog posts, devotions, and novels are all an expression of both these passions.

On any given day, you can find her reading a good book, playing with her German shepherds, Heidi and Kaiser, or drinking coffee with her hubby on the front porch swing. Of course, that's when she's not writing her next cozy mystery or sweet romance.

She is an active member of both American Christian Fiction Writers and Word Weavers International.

Sign up for her newsletter at www.bonitaymccoy.com and

 become part of her newsletter family where she shares giveaways, book recommendations, recipes, and more. Scan to see Bonita's Books!

Suzanne Dodge Nichols grew up in Gulf Breeze, Florida where, during a high school Composition Class, she discovered the rewarding discipline of writing. Through the years, she has found creative expression in almost every genre of the printed word. She especially enjoys blending words and art in ways that can both delight and challenge the observer. She is currently writing a memoir novella honoring the enduring legacy of her maternal grandparents.

With more than 30 years of experience leading Bible Drill, Suzanne has shared her life-long faith in God's Word with the children and youth of her church. During those years, she created *Learn*Love*Live*—a comprehensive, three-cycle curriculum for leading 4th – 6th graders in Children's Bible Drill, and *Bible Basics*—a companion or stand-alone curriculum focused on arming younger children with a greater measure of Bible knowledge, Scripture searching skills, and confidence in God's Word.

Suzanne is a charter member of Word Weavers International North Alabama Chapter. She is published in the *2021, 2022, and 2023 Divine Moments Christmas* anthologies (Grace Publishing) and in seven volumes of the *Short and Sweet* series (Grace Publishing). She is a co-author of *COFFEE with God* (Kerysso Press), a contributor to *Day by Day: 40 Devotionals for Writers & Creative Types* (Southern Christian Writers Conference), and is a 2021 Selah Awards recipient. Suzanne makes her home in Hartselle, Alabama with her husband of 47 years. They have three children and ten grandchildren who live *much* too far away.

Connect with Suzanne at amazon.com/author/suzanne_d_nichols or on the COFFEE with God, Insiders Facebook page.

Lisa Worthey Smith is a long-time Bible student and in-depth Bible study leader, with a passion for pointing people to the Word of God.

She's active in Word Weavers North Alabama, is president of Kerysso Press, a fragrance developer with Reah Fragrance, and an AWSA-certified writing coach. This multiple award-winning and Amazon bestselling author coaches and prays over a number of writers, helping them pursue their God-given talents and writing missions.

Lisa and her high-school sweetheart husband are empty-nesting in north Alabama where she mixes precious oils from around the world, and writes with a cup of Earl Grey beside her "for the generation to come, that a people yet to be created may praise the LORD" Psalm 102:18 (NASB95).

Contact Lisa

Twitter.com@LisaWSmith57

Instagram.com/@LisaW.Smith

Pinterest.com/Lisa Worthey Smith

Website - lisawortheysmithauthor.blogspot.com

Amazon author page - Lisa Worthey Smith

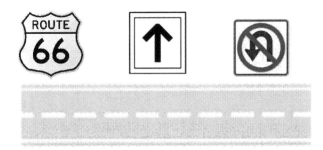

Vol 1 Devotions with an Easter and Spring theme.

Vol 2 Devotions for the month of December, with cookie recipes.

Vol 3 Devotions with stories of love to "Bless Your Heart."

COMPLETE PLAYLIST

"The Great Adventure" by Steven Curtis Chapman

"Every Move I Make, I Make in You" by Integrity Music

"Turn Around" by Matt Maher

"Joy" by Highlands Worship

"Hymn of Heaven" by Phil Wickham

"Thy Word" by Amy Grant

"Trust In You" by Lauren Daigle

"Hold On" by Katy Nichole

"Hard Season" by Matthew West

"Evidence" by Josh Baldwin

"This is Amazing Grace" by Beth Gagliano

"If You Want Me To" by Ginny Owens

"Start a Fire" by Unspoken

"Christ Our Hope in Life and Death" by Keith and Kristyn Getty

"Breathe" by Jonny Diaz

"Look to the Son" by Hillsong

"Jesus the Only Way" by Cameron Keith

"He Paid it All" by Brandon Heath

"Spirit Lead Me" by Hillsong

"Never Lost" by Cece Winans

"Yield Not to Temptation" by Al Green

"I Will Not Fear" by Chris McQuisition

"Tell Your Heart to Beat Again" by Danny Gokey

"Less Like Me" by Zach Williams

"Find Us Faithful" by Steve Green

"Head to Toe" by Christy Nockels

"Available" by Elevation Worship

"The Blessing" by Kari Jobe with Elevation Worship

"Midnight Cry" by Ivan Parker

"While I'm Waiting" by John Waller

"Weary Traveler" by Jordan St. Cyr

A NOTE FROM
BECKY, JUNE, MICHAEL, BONITA, SUZANNE, AND LISA

Every reader and reviewer is an absolute blessing to us.

Thank you!

We hope you enjoyed reading *COFFEE with God on the Road*. If you did, please consider **leaving a quick review** on Amazon, Goodreads, or Barnes and Noble. Just a sentence or two about the book will help other readers find *COFFEE with God* and know if it might be something they would enjoy, too.

I press on toward the goal
for the prize of the upward call of God in Christ Jesus.

Philippians 3:14

MORE ABOUT KERYSSO PRESS

Kerysso Press is a print-on-demand publishing house whose goal is to encourage, edify, and educate. Based on the Greek word κηρύσσω, "kerysso" means to herald, especially a divine truth. This word was used of the public proclamation of the gospel and matters pertaining to it, made by John the Baptist, by Jesus, by the apostles and other Christian teachers.

See **all books published by Kerysso Press** at
KeryssoPress.blogspot.com/books
or scan the QR code
to go directly to the website

Every book sold by Kerysso Press helps deliver Bibles around the world.

Kerysso Press

Made in the USA
Columbia, SC
07 November 2023

25250246R00093